short prayers

FOR PUBLIC WORSHIP

short prayers

FOR PUBLIC WORSHIP

nick FAWCETT

kevin
mayhew

First published in 2003 by
KEVIN MAYHEW LTD
Buxhall, Stowmarket, Suffolk IP14 3BW
Email: info@kevinmayhewltd.com

9 8 7 6 5 4 3 2

ISBN 1 84417 016 0
Catalogue No 1500566

Cover design by Angela Selfe
Typesetting by Louise Selfe
Printed in Great Britain

Contents

Foreword

'Let us pray.' In some quarters those words are greeted with a subconscious sigh. Why? Because the ensuing prayer can at times rival the sermon in length – and, in nonconformist churches at least, that's no mean feat! Longer still were some of the extemporary prayers I used to hear as a boy. In times of open prayer there were always a few individuals whose prayer could be guaranteed to last for anything up to a quarter of an hour, ranging over just about any and every subject, person and place you could imagine. Those who offered such prayers were lovely people – don't get me wrong – deeply committed and unquestionably sincere, but somehow they just couldn't stop their tongues from running away with them.

Lengthy prayers no doubt have their place – I myself have written and prayed a few in my time! – but prayer is an activity in which brevity can be a definite virtue. We have that on the highest authority, Jesus himself urging people 'not to pile up pointless phrases as the Gentiles do, imagining God will listen to them because of their many words' (Matthew 6:7; own paraphrase). Paradoxically, those who communicate most effectively are often those who say the least, and vice versa.

Many of us probably already apply the words of Jesus in our devotional lives, albeit inadvertently, offering up brief single-sentence prayers to succinctly express the mood of a moment rather than attempting anything more eloquent. Partly this is down to constraints on time, but it's also because it feels natural. Prayer, after all, is meant to be a conversation, not a monologue, but if God is going to speak he needs the opportunity to get a word in.

In the context of public worship, other factors come into play. With the best will in the world, many will find their attention starting to wander if prayers go on for too long. I speak from experience, having come perilously close on a few occasions to nodding off during particularly loquacious intercessions. With such considerations in mind, I took, during my time in the ministry, to using two or three short prayers of intercession, much as Anglicans and Catholics use brief collects rather than a single 'long prayer'. Instead of attempting to cover every issue in the world, I focused on a few needs and situations, tying these in as far as possible with the theme of the service.

The prayers in this book – some drawn and adapted from my earlier books *Daily Prayer* and *Prayers for all Seasons*, and others newly written

– are not intended to serve as the principal prayers in a service of public worship. They are designed, rather, to sum up and commit to God a particular area of life or faith, and as such they can be used in different ways and at different points in the service. Some lend themselves to the close of worship and others to its opening. Some will fit well at the end of a sermon, others in consecrating an offering, others again as prayers of approach, and others still as short intercessions or expressions of praise and confession. You may find yet other ways of using them. Arranged in alphabetical sections, they cover a wide range of themes, spanning daily life and relationships, the journey of discipleship, morning and evening prayers, the Christian seasons, sorrow and death, joy and thanksgiving, and much more. All, though, have one thing in common: they are offered as a way of simply, concisely, yet sincerely committing our lives and our worship to God in prayer. I hope and pray that they may help do just that.

NICK FAWCETT

Call of God

see also Word of God

1   Gracious God, for your call to be your people and your invitation to share in the work of your kingdom, we praise you. Help us to respond wholeheartedly and to live up to the trust you have placed in us, through Jesus Christ our Lord. Amen.

2   Gracious God, give us strength to answer your call. May we be ready, like so many before us, to respond in faith and follow where you might lead, to the glory of your name. Amen.

3   Living God, teach us to hear your cry in the groans of the hungry, the suffering of the sick, the plight of the homeless and the sorrow of the bereaved; to hear your call in the misery of the lonely, the despair of the oppressed, the plea of the weak and the helplessness of the poor. Teach us to listen and to respond, in the name of Christ. Amen.

4   Sovereign God, you have called us to be your people: help us, then, to live as your children, to the glory of your name. Amen.

5   Loving God, there are times in our lives when you call us to tasks that seem beyond us, tasks we would rather avoid. We hear your voice but feel unable to meet the challenge and our natural inclination is to run away. Remind us that when you ask us to do something, you give us the strength to do it. Give us courage, then, to respond when you call, knowing that, however things may seem, you are always able to transform them in ways far beyond our expectations. Amen.

Voice of God

6   Gracious God, when we listen for your voice, save us from deciding what we want you to say before you have a chance to speak. Amen.

7   Loving God, draw close to us and help us to draw nearer to you. Speak to us and help us to hear. Challenge us and help us to respond. Enthuse us with the wonder of your love, and so may joy and peace fill our hearts, now and for evermore. Amen.

8   Gracious God, help us to hear again your still small voice, your word even in the silence, and so to recognise that, though sometimes we may not see it, you are always there and always active, through Jesus Christ our Lord. Amen.

9   Lord of all, teach us to listen to your voice before we speak, and to seek your will before attempting to impose our own. Amen.

10   Gracious God, grant us the humility we need to hear your voice and the faith we need to respond. Amen.

11   Living God, open our hearts to what you would say even when we would rather not hear it. Open our lives to what you would have us do, even when we would rather not do it. Help us to respond to your disturbing, challenging word, in the name of Christ. Amen.

12   Sovereign God, guide us in the reading and understanding of your word, until it becomes so much a part of us that your voice is heard through all we are and do, to the glory of your name. Amen.

13   Gracious God, speak to us now and help us to listen. Open our ears to all the ways your voice may come, and then, like Samuel, teach us to respond in faith, for Jesus' sake. Amen.

Christian seasons

Advent and Christmas

14   Lord Jesus Christ, prepare our hearts to welcome you now, and so may we be ready to welcome you when you come again. Amen.

15   Loving God, teach us that your gracious purpose goes back to the beginning of time, and that it will endure until the end of time, and beyond. Amen.

16   Lord Jesus Christ, teach us to anticipate your return by preparing the way for your coming; to catch a glimpse of your kingdom through living by its values today. Live in us now, so that the day may come when we live with you and all your people for all eternity, your will complete and your promise fulfilled. In your name we ask it. Amen.

17   Lord Jesus Christ, we look forward to that day when your kingdom shall come and you are all in all. Until then, we will trust in you, secure in your love, confident in your eternal purpose, assured that your will shall be done. To you be praise and glory, now and for evermore. Amen.

18   Living God, teach us that the joyful message proclaimed at Bethlehem all those years ago is good news for us today, here and now. Amen.

19   Lord Jesus, child in the manger, man on the cross, risen Saviour, Lord of all, be born in us today. Amen.

Epiphany *see* **Light in our darkness**

Lent *see also* **Confession and Forgiveness**

20   Living God, cleanse us from within and purge us of everything that keeps us from you. Amen.

21   Lord Jesus Christ, teach us when to say 'yes' and when to say 'no', and help us not only to take those decisions but also to stick to them once taken. Amen.

22   Sovereign God, for the many ways we fail to live as members of your people, forgive us. Guard us from temptation and teach us to live by your Spirit. Amen.

23   Gracious God, teach us to wrestle with our sin, our doubts, our fears and our weaknesses, and, in battling with those, may we find we have taken hold of you, through Christ our Lord. Amen.

24   Loving God, teach us to see beneath the surface and to recognise that good and evil bring their own reward. So may we live with integrity, intent on doing your will. Amen.

Holy Week

25   Lord Jesus Christ, you gave so much; help us to give to you, if only a little, in return. Amen.

26   Lord Jesus Christ, you gave your all so that we might have life; you counted yourself as nothing so that we might rejoice in the wonder of your love; you endured agony of body, mind and spirit, so that we might receive mercy and know the peace that only you can give. Help us today to recognise more clearly everything you did for us, and so inspire us to give a little of ourselves in return. Teach us to walk the way of the cross and to bear the cost gladly for the joy set before us, for your name's sake. Amen.

Easter *see also* Evil, triumph over

27   Living God, teach us that the gospel not only sounds good news; it is good news! Amen.

28   Lord Jesus Christ, as you rose victorious over death, so may hope, faith and love continue to triumph in our lives over everything that conspires against them. Amen.

29   Lord Jesus Christ, may the message of your glorious resurrection continue to stir our hearts and change lives today, just as it has spoken to so many across the years. Amen.

Ascension

30   Lord Jesus Christ, remind us of all that you are and equip us to live to your glory, until that day when we kneel in your presence and join in the worship of heaven, to the glory of your name. Amen.

31   Lord Jesus Christ, may our lives as well as our lips proclaim you as King of kings and Lord of lords, to the glory of your name. Amen.

Pentecost

32   Holy Spirit, unpredictable as the wind, unquenchable as fire, yet gentle as a dove: come now and breathe new energy into our lives and new life into our souls, by your gracious power. Amen.

Trinity Sunday

33   Let the love of the Father course through our veins. Let the goodness of Christ pulse through our bodies. Let the power of the Spirit flow through our souls. Let the wonder of God resonate through our minds. Glory be to God, Father, Son and Holy Spirit, now and for all eternity. Amen.

34   Loving God, equip us through the inner presence of your Holy Spirit, enrich us through the redeeming grace of Christ, and encourage us through the daily experience of your fatherly love. Strengthen our service, deepen our faith and enliven our commitment so that we may live to your praise and glory. Amen.

35   Sovereign God, Father, Son and Holy Spirit, teach us to live with mystery, and to celebrate each day our innumerable experiences of your love. Amen.

36   Mighty God, Father, Son and Holy Spirit, save us from bringing you down to our level, from limiting you to our narrow horizons and flawed understanding. Help us instead to rise up to new heights, catching a glimpse of your sovereign power and the way you are able to work in our lives and the lives of all. Amen.

All Saints' Day

37   Living God, encourage us through all who have gone before us,
        so that we, in turn, may encourage those who travel after us,
        along the way of Christ. Amen.

Commitment

see also Growing in grace

38 Lord Jesus Christ, teach us to take up our cross, but also to celebrate your gift of new life. Amen.

39 Loving God, teach us not just to know about your invitation to meet with Christ, but to respond and know him for ourselves. Amen.

40 Lord Jesus Christ, you chose to identify yourself with us in all our frailty and sinfulness. Help us gladly to identify ourselves with you, proud to bear your name. Amen.

41 Living God, fill our hearts with your love and draw near in your grace, so that our faith may stay as fresh today and every day as when it first began. Amen.

42 Gracious God, always you remember us. Teach us to remember you. Amen.

43 Lord Jesus Christ, may your power flow in us, through us and from us, to the glory of your name. Amen.

44 Loving God, kindle the spark of faith within us until the fire of your love burns brightly within our hearts, blazing for your glory. Amen.

45 Gracious God, when the spark of faith starts to flicker and the fire of commitment grows cold, rekindle in us the joy with which we first started out, so that we may awake each day with hope in our heart and live each moment rejoicing in your love, to the glory of your name. Amen.

Living for Jesus

46 Gracious God, may our vision be clear, our commitment strong and our faith constant, and so may your light shine through us, to the glory of your name. Amen.

47   Sovereign God, teach us to base our faith not simply on the testimony of others, but on our own experience of Christ. Amen.

48   Lord Jesus Christ, save us from simply knowing about you; help us truly to know you as our Lord, Saviour and friend, through your grace. Amen.

Walking with Jesus *see also* Discipleship, journey of

49   Lord Jesus, help us to walk as closely with you as you walk with us. Amen.

50   Lord Jesus Christ, help us to follow in your footsteps, walking where you might lead us, trusting in your guidance. Teach us that wherever you ask us to go, you will be walking with us, matching us stride for stride. Amen.

Rededication

51   Almighty God, we commit to you not simply a part but all of life, asking that you will take who and what we are, and everything we do, and dedicate it to your service, for your name's sake. Amen.

52   Gracious God, teach us to be as committed to you as you are to us. Amen.

53   Gracious God, take our faith, flawed though it is, our love, poor though it may be, and our commitment, with all its imperfections, and use us in your service to make known your gracious purpose, through Jesus Christ our Lord. Amen.

Confession and forgiveness

see also Christian seasons: Lent

54   Gracious God, help us to acknowledge our sins not only to you but to those we sin against, and help us to say sorry not only through our words but through our actions, in the name of Christ. Amen.

55   Lord Jesus Christ, teach us to be honest with you, with ourselves and with others, and so may we know the peace of a clear conscience and a right relationship with you and others. Amen.

56   Gracious God, give us the wisdom and humility we need to recognise our mistakes, to acknowledge them openly, to seek forgiveness, and, where possible, to make amends. Amen.

57   Almighty God, forgive us the smallness of our vision and the feebleness of our faith. Open our eyes to the wonder of all that you are, and may that knowledge sustain and inspire us all our days. Amen.

58   Lord Jesus Christ, teach us not simply to turn from our old ways, but to embrace the new, celebrating life as you desire and living to your praise and glory. Amen.

Confessing

59   Lord Jesus Christ, we know how we have failed you and we know how we ought to serve you. By your grace help us to move from the one closer to the other. Amen.

60   Lord, forgive what we are and have been, and bless what we shall be, to the glory of your name. Amen.

61   Merciful God, for all in our lives that is but should not be, and for all that is not but should be, forgive us, through Jesus Christ, our Lord. Amen.

62   Lord Jesus Christ, we have failed you, we have failed ourselves, we have failed others. Forgive us and help us to live in a way that is true to all. Amen.

63   Almighty God, pardon us our past mistakes, deliver us from present folly, and lead us forward in the way of life eternal. Amen.

Receiving forgiveness

64   Loving God, we thank you that you expect no recompense for our sins; otherwise we could never repay the debt. We praise you that you seek simply our acceptance of your love and acknowledgement of your grace. Freely you have given, freely we receive, in the name of Christ. Amen.

65   Gracious God, always watching, always loving, always caring, always ready to forgive and forget: we give you praise, in the name of Christ. Amen.

66   Sovereign God, when we do wrong, give us courage to acknowledge it before you and others, so that we may know your forgiveness and open a way to the healing of the wounds our mistakes have caused. Amen.

67   Gracious God, just as we are, we come, committing ourselves to your loving mercy, through Jesus Christ our Lord. Amen.

68   Lord Jesus Christ, touch our lives with your healing forgiveness, and put a new heart and a right spirit within us, so that we may truly love you and faithfully serve you, to the glory of your name. Amen.

Forgiving others

69   Loving God, teach us to recognise how much we have been forgiven and so help us to reach out to others in turn, ready to show mercy, to forgive and to forget, for your name's sake. Amen.

70   Lord Jesus Christ, as you have forgiven us, teach us to forgive others, wholly and unreservedly, for your name's sake. Amen.

Creation

Stewardship of

71 Living God, teach us to show our gratitude for all you have created, not merely through words but through stewarding it wisely and handing it on intact for future generations to enjoy in turn. Amen.

72 Sovereign God, teach us to see the world not as a trinket or a plaything but as a priceless treasure – an heirloom held in trust. So teach us to live wisely and responsibly, in harmony with you and all you have made. Amen.

73 Loving God, forgive us for taking your many gifts for granted – forgetting, squandering and even abusing them. Help us to rejoice in all you have given and to steward it faithfully, to your glory. Amen.

Wonder of

74 Gracious God, open our eyes to the loveliness of this world and, in honouring your creation, may we honour you. Amen.

75 Sovereign God, for the wonder of the universe that continues to astound us, for the beauty of the earth that still enthrals us, for the miracle of creation that yet inspires us and for the gift of life that each day you give us, we offer our joyful worship and heartfelt thanksgiving, in the name of Christ. Amen.

76 In the grandeur of creation but also its simplicity, in its power but also its gentleness, in all we know but all that yet remains a mystery, teach us, O Lord, to glimpse something of you, the sovereign hand behind it all. Amen.

Daily life

Finding God in

77 Living God, go with us back to the daily round of life, and may what we have shared here transform all we do and experience there. Amen.

78 Lord Jesus Christ, as you have turned the water of our lives into wine, help us to glimpse the special in the ordinary, the first in the last and the possible in the impossible. Help us to bring out the best in every person and situation, to the glory of your name. Amen.

79 Lord Jesus Christ, send us back to the daily business of life with eyes open to see you, ears open to hear you, minds open to receive you and hearts open to serve you, for your name's sake. Amen.

80 Sovereign God, go with us and thrill us afresh each day by the extent of your love, the awesomeness of your power, the generosity of your mercy and the graciousness of your purpose. Amen.

Serving God in

81 Loving God, lead us out into the world, renewed in vigour, rekindled in hope, reborn in faith and resolved in purpose. Send us back to live and work for you, sharing your love and living your life, through Jesus Christ our Lord. Amen.

82 Loving God, send us back into the world renewed in hope and restored in faith, to live and work for you. Amen.

83 Lord Jesus Christ, may your grace redeem us, your power renew us, your example inspire us, and your love shine from us. Send us out, renewed in faith, to walk each day in your way and to make you known, to the glory of your name. Amen.

84 Living God, help us to live each day for you so that your life may shine each day through us, to the glory of your name. Amen.

85   Living God, send us out with love in our hearts, light in our eyes and life in our souls, to proclaim each day what you have done for us and to celebrate each moment that which you have given. Amen.

86   Lord Jesus Christ, help us to worship you not just for these few moments or in one small part of our lives, but in all our words and deeds – through the people we are and the lives we lead, the praise we bring you and the service we offer. In your name we ask it. Amen.

Death and new life

see also Christian seasons: Easter; New beginnings

87   Living God, teach us to look beyond the apparent finality of death to the new life you hold for all your people, and help us to rest secure in the knowledge that nothing can finally separate us or those we love from your sovereign purpose in Jesus Christ our Lord. Amen.

88   Lord Jesus Christ, may new life be born within us this and every day, and may your life-giving hope sustain us through the joys and sorrows of this world until that time when we pass through the shadow of death into the light of your eternal kingdom. Amen.

89   Sovereign God, instead of fearing death, teach us eagerly to anticipate your kingdom and the new life we will celebrate within it, through Jesus Christ our Lord. Amen.

90   Living God, teach us to recognise that death is not so much an end as a new beginning, leading us into fullness of life, enduring for all eternity. Amen.

91   Lord Jesus Christ, just as death could not hold you teach us that the grave can never hold us, for your purpose continues, your grace persists, and your love endures not just today but for all eternity. In that knowledge, teach us to live life and meet death in the same way: in quiet confidence and firm hope, through Jesus Christ our Lord. Amen.

92   Living God, where death casts its shadow over life, seeming to block out all rays of hope, remind us of your promised kingdom in which there will be no more night, nor need for lamp or sun, for your light will be all in all, shining for evermore. Amen.

Discipleship, journey of

see also Guidance; Trust

93   Gracious God, whenever we lose our way, call us back and help us to turn again to the living way, through Jesus Christ our Lord. Amen.

94   Living God, send us back to our journey of discipleship redeemed in love, renewed in faith, restored in strength and refreshed in spirit, in the name of the risen Christ who goes before us. Amen.

95   May the grace of God always surround us, enriching our lives, seasoning our words and shaping our actions, and so may we live always to his praise and glory, through Jesus Christ our Lord. Amen.

96   Lord Jesus Christ, teach us what it means to be a disciple, and, by your grace, help us to respond and to be followers of your way, to the glory of your name. Amen.

97   The Lord watch over us, his hands below, his arms around and his Spirit within, and so may he lead us this and every day as we travel along life's chequered path. In the name of Christ. Amen.

98   May the word of God guide our footsteps, the power of God equip us for service, the grace of God renew us and the love of God surround us always. May Christ be our constant companion on the path of discipleship, until our journey is over and we meet with God face to face, secure in the joy of his everlasting kingdom. In his name we ask it. Amen.

99   Merciful Lord, with hearts at peace we return to the journey of life, the past put behind us, the future full of promise. Receive our praise, in the name of Christ. Amen.

100   Lord Jesus Christ, teach us not just to acknowledge you as Lord but also to follow you in faith and to walk wherever you would lead, to the glory of your name. Amen.

101   Lord Jesus Christ, you have shown us the way to life and invited us to follow. Freely we respond, in your name. Amen.

102   Sovereign God, before all, above all, within all, beyond all: go with us now and remain with us always, through Jesus Christ our Lord. Amen.

103   Living God, embrace us in your arms, encircle us with your grace, enfold us in your love, and lead us safely onward until our journey is over and you are all in all. Amen.

Perseverance

104   Living God, help us to meet difficulties and disappointments with confidence, knowing that you will equip us to respond to whatever may be asked of us. Amen.

105   Living God, by your grace, equip, enable and enthuse us, so that we may faithfully walk the way of Christ, and finish what we have started. Amen.

106   Lord Jesus Christ, inspire us through your love and the great company of those who have gone before us, to persevere and run the race, to the glory of your name. Amen.

107   Sovereign God, equip us with faith, hope, courage, resilience, enthusiasm and dedication, so that we may walk the path of discipleship faithfully, through good or ill, to the glory of your name. Amen.

108   Living God, when what you ask seems beyond us, help us to trust in your purpose, and if we meet with failure, teach us not to lose faith but to try and keep on trying, in Christ's name. Amen.

109   Living God, open our eyes to the great adventure of faith and to the unfathomable mysteries of your purpose, and so help us to live as pilgrims, travelling together in hope. Amen.

110   Lord Jesus Christ, help us to walk the journey to which you have called us, keeping faith in your saving purpose. When we grow weary, revive us; when we go astray, direct us; when we lose heart, inspire us, and when we turn back reprove us. Keep

us travelling ever onwards, trusting in your guidance and certain that you will be there at our journey's end, to welcome us home into your eternal kingdom. In your name, we ask it. Amen.

111   Living God, hold on to us, keep us steady, and direct our foot-steps and, if we stumble, lead us on to the way of life once more so that we may continue safely until our journey's end. In the name of Christ we ask it. Amen.

112   Lord Jesus Christ, though the journey is long and we encounter obstacles along the way, help us to keep on searching to know you better, until that day when we enter your kingdom and meet you face to face. Amen.

113   Lord, whatever we may face, teach us that your power is sufficient for all our needs. Teach us, then, to walk in faith, confident that you will show us the way forward. Amen.

114   Sovereign God, rekindle our vision, revive our faith and renew our resolve to take up our cross and follow where you would lead us. Show us the way in Christ and give us faith to follow, for his name's sake. Amen.

115   Sovereign God, when we are led astray, call us back and help us to walk your way more faithfully, to our journey's end. Amen.

116   Sovereign God, renew our faith, revive our hope, restore our trust, rekindle our vision, and so may we serve you in quiet confidence, this day and always. Amen.

Looking forward

117   Lord Jesus Christ, teach us to travel light and to let go of all that may encumber us on our journey. So may we walk your way faithfully to the end, to the glory of your name. Amen.

118   Living God, we thank you that, wherever we are, whatever we face, you are with us, through Christ, constantly by our side, travelling with us and looking to lead us forward into new experiences of your love. Receive our praise, through Jesus Christ our Lord. Amen.

119   Sovereign God, open our hearts to all you have yet to say, do and teach. Help us, whoever we may be, to recognise that, however far we have come, our journey has only just begun, and so may we continue to explore the wonder of your love and the mystery of your gracious purpose, this day and for evermore. Amen.

120   Loving God, teach us to walk with you, confident that, though we do not know the way, you will guide our footsteps to our journey's end. Amen.

Evening

121   Living God, speak to us through everything life has brought us today, good and bad, pleasure or pain, and so help us to be better equipped to serve and love you in the days ahead, to the glory of your name. Amen.

122   Eternal God, though darkness falls and night comes upon us, keep us always in the light of your love and the radiance of your presence, through Jesus Christ our Lord. Amen.

123   Mighty God, for all the ways you have been with us this day, protecting, providing, instructing, inspiring, we give you our praise, in the name of Christ. Amen.

124   Gracious God, for all that this day has brought us we offer you our thanks. Recognised or unrecognised, seen or unseen, you have been there, taking our hand to lead us forward. In the knowledge of all you have done and will yet do, we will take our rest, in peace and quiet confidence. Amen.

125   The Lord fill us with light and enfold us in his love, this night and for evermore. Amen.

126   Lord Jesus Christ, the same yesterday, today and tomorrow, we thank you for all we have experienced today, we trust you for all we shall experience tomorrow. Always you are faithful, worthy of honour and adulation. Receive, then, our joyful worship, in the name of Christ. Amen.

127   Gracious God, grant rest for our bodies through this night and rest for our souls always. Amen.

128   Lord Jesus Christ, enfold us in your peace, encircle us with your love, and so may we pass this night and live our days in quietness of mind and tranquillity of spirit, through Jesus Christ our Lord. Amen.

129   Loving God, thank you for all we have done this day and forgive us for all we should have done but failed to do. Amen.

_____ Evil, triumph over _____

see also Christian seasons: Easter

130   Lord of all, despite everything that conspires against it, help us to hold on to the conviction that good will finally conquer evil, and your love ultimately triumph over all. Amen.

131   Teach us, Lord, that you are constantly at work, striving against everything that frustrates your will and denies your love. Teach us to hold on to those moments in life when wrongs are righted and justice is done at last. Above all, teach us to look at the cross of Christ, and to draw strength from the victory of love over what had seemed to be the triumph of evil. Amen.

132   Lord Jesus Christ, for the victory you have won over sin and death, and the victories you continue to win in our lives, receive our praise. Amen.

133   Lord Jesus Christ, you faced up to evil, even though it cost you your life to conquer it: give us wisdom to know when we must stand up for our principles, and then give us courage to stand firm, for your name's sake. Amen.

134   Sovereign God, teach us that, even where evil has done its worst, where darkness seems victorious and where hopelessness seems unrelieved, you are still there, working in all things for good, nothing able finally to frustrate your gracious purpose in Jesus Christ our Lord. Amen.

135   Lord Jesus Christ, you took on your shoulders the crushing weight of human sinfulness – and nailed it to a cross. You endured the full force of human hatred – and overcame it with love. You entered the apparent finality of death – and through it opened the way to life. You took on the powers of evil – and triumphed over them through good. To you be praise and glory, now and for ever. Amen.

Faithfulness of God

see also Guidance; Praise; Presence of God; Trust

136   Gracious God, though we forget you, do not forget us. Meet with us and help us to glimpse again your glory. Amen.

137   Living God, you have given us enough and more than enough. Receive our praise, in Christ's name. Amen.

138   Lord Jesus Christ, we thank you that, though we are faithful to you in so little, you are faithful in so much; that, though we repeatedly change our tune, your love never fails. To you be praise and glory, now and for ever. Amen.

139   Almighty God, through all things you remember us; help us to remember you, in Jesus' name. Amen.

140   God of grace, forgive us; Lord of creation, remake us; ruler of history, direct our path. Be a rock to support us, a shield to protect us, and a fortress to surround us. Amen.

141   Gracious God, for the constancy of your love, the faithfulness of your guidance and the certainty of your help, receive our praise, in the name of Christ. Amen.

142   Gracious God, we rejoice in the knowledge that, though we so easily give up on you, you will never give up on us. For that great truth, we praise you, in the name of Christ. Amen.

143   Loving God, wherever we are, wherever we go, whatever we do, however we feel, we know that you will be with us, to hold, to heal, to guide and to bless. So, we will go in peace, assured of your unfailing love. Amen.

144   Sovereign God, faithful and true, in you we put our trust, confident that what you have promised will come to fruition. To you be praise and glory, now and always, through Jesus Christ our Lord. Amen.

Yesterday, today, for ever *see also* **Time**

145   Lord Jesus Christ, teach us that whatever today may hold and whatever tomorrow might bring, the future is secure, for you are with us, the same yesterday, today and for ever. Help us, then, to live each moment with you, in quiet confidence and joyful celebration, knowing that we are yours and you are ours, for all eternity. Amen.

146   Sovereign God, we look back in wonder, we look forward in confidence, and so we look to you now in worship, through Jesus Christ, our Lord. Amen.

147   Gracious God, day after day, year after year, you are there to hold on to us. Day after day, year after year, help us to hold on to you, by the grace of Christ. Amen.

148   Living God, ever old, ever new, speak to us and through us of your great love in Jesus Christ, always the same yet never exhausted. Amen.

149   Living God, for the help you have given and the assistance you are always ready to give, receive our praise, in the name of Christ. Amen.

150   Loving God, just as you have provided over the years for our deepest needs, so help us today to trust for the future, knowing that your love will not fail. Amen.

151   God of past, present and future, help us to remember all you have done, to rejoice in all you are doing, and to trust in all you will yet do. Teach us to put our hand in yours and to walk with you wherever you may lead, knowing that you will walk by our side, this day and always. Amen.

In change and uncertainty

152   Living God, in all the fluctuating fortunes of this life, teach us that your love and the life you hold for us in Christ, endure for ever. Amen.

153 Living God, in this uncertain and fleeting world, help us to keep our eyes fixed on you, knowing that, though all else may change, you will not. Amen.

154 Living God, teach us that, though others may prove false, you will stay true, your promises sure, your love constant and your mercy unfailing. Amen.

155 Lord, even when we cannot see you, when life seems dark and hope seems to be in vain, teach us to keep faith with you, knowing that you will keep faith with us. Amen.

156 Sovereign God, hold on to us in all the changes and chances of life. Help us to put our hand in yours, knowing that you are there, sharing our experience and able to see us safely through. Amen.

157 Sovereign God, when we can carry on no longer, our burdens too heavy to bear, take hold of us, take hold of them, and carry all in your loving arms, through Jesus Christ our Lord. Amen.

158 Merciful God, encircle us, nurture us, guide and protect us, for we are weak and foolish children. In your great love, stay close and watch over us always. Amen.

Faith in action

159   Living God, remind us that worship without action, faith without deeds, is like a well without water, a book without words – promising much yet yielding nothing. Teach us, then, to practise our faith rather than simply profess it, for your name's sake. Amen.

160   The God who called us here is sending us out, to turn words into deeds, worship into service and vision into reality. Together we have celebrated the faith; now let us share it, in the name of Christ. Amen.

161   Living God, grant that not only our words but everything we are and do may be offered to you as a living prayer, in the name of Christ. Amen.

162   Living God, save us from a life that proclaims one thing, but displays another. Amen.

163   Living God, teach us to show in our lives the loyalty we declare with our lips. Amen.

164   Living God, you have made yourself real to us in Christ: help us now to make you real to others, demonstrating the reality of our faith through the people we are, the service we offer and the lives we lead, to the glory of your name. Amen.

165   Lord Jesus Christ, as you have shown your love to us, help us to show our love to others. May our deeds speak as clearly as our words, testifying to your grace and mercy, to the glory of your name. Amen.

166   Lord Jesus Christ, by your grace, help us not just to talk of loyalty but to show it, to you and to others, now and always. Amen.

167   Lord Jesus Christ, deliver us from a flabby couch-potato faith, so out of condition that it is doomed finally to collapse and die. Teach us to put faith into action, so that it may be stretched and grow, and equip us for service in your kingdom, through Christ our Lord. Amen.

168   Lord Jesus Christ, save us from simply talking about faith, from meaning to do what is good. Help us to turn concern into compassion, sympathy into service, aim into action, resolve into reality, and so may we be the people you want us to be, to your glory. Amen.

169   Lord Jesus Christ, teach us to live each moment in such a manner that we would be happy for you to walk in upon us. Help us to honour you through all we are and do, and thus to share in the growth of your kingdom, on earth as it is in heaven. Amen.

170   Loving God, go with us now and help us to offer the worship you most desire – to do justice, to love kindness and to walk humbly with you every step of the way, in the name of Christ. Amen.

Grace of God

see also Love: God's love of us

171   Living God, teach us that your grace is wider than we can begin to imagine, and your love wonderful beyond words. Amen.

172   Gracious God, as we consider our response to others, teach us what it cost you to bring life for all through your Son – the greatest gift there could be. Amen.

173   Gracious God, may your love continue to astonish us, your grace to captivate us, your strength to sustain us, and your call to surprise us. Go with us, now and for evermore. Amen.

174   Merciful God, your gracious love keeps no score of wrongs, no record of past mistakes. Teach us to let go in turn, and to believe the best of others as you have believed the best of us. Amen.

175   Living God, flawed and fallible though we are, work within us by your grace to do your will and fulfil your purpose, through Christ our Saviour. Amen.

176   Lord Jesus Christ, take what we are and have been and, by your renewing, redeeming touch, direct what we shall be, to the glory of your name. Amen.

177   Lord Jesus Christ, though we deserve so little, teach us that you are always ready to give much, provided we are ready to ask and to receive. Amen.

178   Lord Jesus Christ, whenever we question our worth, teach us that you believe in us totally, enough even to die for us so that we might enter into your kingdom, and in that knowledge may we live each day, at one with ourselves and at one with you. Amen.

179   Loving God, we have no claim on your love, no entitlement to your mercy, and yet your nature is always to forgive and forget. Open our hearts to your grace, and help us to receive the new life you long to give us. Amen.

180   Sovereign God, for your grace that thrills our hearts, your mercy that transforms our minds, your peace that floods our souls and your love that flows through our lives, receive our praise. Amen.

181   Sovereign God, we owe you everything, yet, by your grace, we owe you nothing! Great is your name and greatly to be praised! Amen.

Growing in grace

182   Lord Jesus Christ, when our faith is weak, strengthen it; when it is shallow, nurture it; when it is flawed, correct it; and when it is partial, complete it, for your name's sake. Amen.

183   Gracious God, make us generous of heart, warm of spirit, forgiving in attitude and sunny of disposition. Amen.

184   Gracious God, take what is, show us what can be, and direct what shall be. Amen.

185   Gracious God, though we can never hope to live as faithfully as we ought to, help us to try. Amen.

186   Living God, as the dew falls in the morning, so may your grace descend upon us. As the sun bathes all in its life-giving light, so may the radiance of Christ shine in our hearts. As the wind blows where it will, so may the breath of the Spirit move freely within us. Take what we are and use us for your glory. Amen.

187   Loving God, touch our hearts, our mouths, ourselves, so that our thoughts, our words and our deeds may reach out to you and to others and bring glory to your name. Amen.

188   Living God, grant us the wisdom of years and the enthusiasm of childhood, the discernment of adulthood and the innocence of youth. Help us to rediscover the child in us and so grow to maturity in you. Amen.

189   Living God, teach us always to seek for understanding, and always to recognise how little we have understood. Amen.

190   Living God, teach us that, whatever we have learned about you and however established our faith may be, there is still more to discover and further to grow. Open our life, then, to new horizons, through Christ our Lord. Amen.

191   Lord Jesus Christ, help us always to remember that you are able to change not just other people's lives but ours too. Renew us day by day through your redeeming grace. Amen.

192   Gracious Lord, be a blessing to us, leading us in the way of peace, wisdom, love and humility, so that we, in turn, may be a blessing to others, to the glory of your name. Amen.

193   Lord Jesus Christ, nourish us through your word, nurture us through your grace, feed us through your Spirit, fill us with your love, for your name's sake. Amen.

194   Lord Jesus Christ, open our hearts to your searching presence, and teach us to respond to your challenging word, however unsettling that might be. Amen.

195   Lord Jesus Christ, save us from thinking we have arrived in our faith. Show us that, however far we have come, there is always further to go and more to be revealed, for your name's sake. Amen.

196   Loving God, make a difference to us, so that we may make a difference to others. Amen.

197   Prince of Peace, heal us. Lamb of God, redeem us. Shepherd of the sheep, guard us. Light of the world, lead us. Lord Jesus Christ, touch our lives by your grace, and help us to live and work for you, to your glory. Amen.

198   Sovereign God, open our hearts afresh to the wonder of your presence, the awesomeness of your power, the breadth of your love and the extent of your purpose. So may we live each day to the glory of your name. Amen.

Closer to God

199   Lord Jesus Christ, draw close to us and help us to draw closer to you, so that we may know and love you better and follow more faithfully as your disciples, now and always. Amen.

200   Living God, when we forget you, fail you and wander far from your side, draw near by your grace, and open our hearts afresh to your love, through Jesus Christ our Lord. Amen.

201   Lord Jesus Christ, help us to turn from everything that leads us astray, and to focus on you and your will, for your name's sake. Amen.

202   Sovereign God, by your grace help us to know you better, to love you more fully and to serve you more completely, day by day. Amen.

203   Sovereign God, give us today a deeper sense of who and what you are, and may we acknowledge your greatness through word and deed, to the glory of your name. Amen.

204   Gracious God, nurture the seed of faith within us. Help us to grow closer to you and to Christ, and so cultivate within us the fruits you hunger to see, through the grace of Jesus Christ, our Lord. Amen.

More like Jesus

205   Loving God, take what we are and remould us by your grace, so that we will bear the image of Christ within us, and live to his glory. Amen.

206   May the joy of Christ shine in our eyes, the compassion of Christ reach out through our hands, the word of Christ fall from our tongues and the love of Christ flow from our hearts. Amen.

207   Living God, help us before all else to clothe ourselves with Christ and so make him known through word and deed, to the glory of his name. Amen.

208   Lord Jesus Christ, help us to grow in you so that something of you may grow in us, for your name's sake. Amen.

209   Lord Jesus Christ, make us one with you, just as you are one with the Father. Remake us in his image, so that something of him may shine from us, to the glory of his name. Amen.

210   Lord Jesus Christ, renew, remake, remould, reshape us. By your grace, redeem and restore, reclaim and refashion, and so help us to live as your people. Amen.

211   Lord Jesus Christ, teach us that if we would be in you, you first must be in us. Amen.

212   Sovereign God, Lord of creation, remake us in your image and save us from trying to mould you to our own. Amen.

Guidance

213   Loving God, go with us now, and through all the uncertainties of life may we glimpse your presence, a beacon of hope and a signpost along the way. Amen.

214   The Lord watch over us, this and every day; the Lord guide our footsteps and keep us from evil; the Lord grant us health and strength, joy and fulfilment, our whole life long. Amen.

215   Everlasting God, send us out into the days ahead, confident that, whatever they may bring, you will be with us, and that your loving purpose will not fail. Amen.

216   Gracious God, we praise you for the assurance that, though we may sometimes lose sight of you, you will never lose sight of us. Watch over us, and lead us safely through our journey of life. Amen.

217   Gracious God, when we are uncertain of the way ahead, give us guidance, and when we feel discouraged, give us fresh inspiration. May the knowledge of your unfailing love give us confidence that, whatever problems we might face and whatever sorrows might befall us, we shall still find reason to believe in the future and to hope. Amen.

218   Gracious God, show us where we have lost our way and help us to learn from past mistakes. Show us where our loyalties are still divided and, by your grace, help us to change. Show us the path to life, and help us to walk it more faithfully, for Christ's sake. Amen.

219   Lord Jesus Christ, guide our thinking, our living and our praying, that we may discern your will, follow your way and receive your blessing. Amen.

220   Loving God, through all that life brings and in all the challenges we face, help us to see the way forward and to follow where you would lead us. Amen.

221   Living God, show us the doors you have opened and teach us to walk through them in faith, trusting in your guidance and power, this day and always. Amen.

222   Gracious God, go with us now, protect us from evil, deliver us from temptation, and help us to walk in the way of Christ, this and every day, for his name's sake. Amen.

223   Gracious God, may your light guide our footsteps along the pathway of life. May your hand rest upon us and your love always enfold us, and so lead us safely onwards to know and love you better, to the glory of your name. Amen.

Purpose of God *see also* Discipleship, journey of: Perseverance

224   Living God, because of or despite us, for or against us, with our help or our hindrance, may your will be done in our lives and all things, by the grace of Christ. Amen.

225   Living God, open our eyes to all you are doing now, and so may we glimpse all you will yet do, through Christ our Lord. Amen.

Wisdom of God

226   Gracious God, grant us the wisdom of advancing years, together with the innocent enthusiasm of a little child and, by your grace, help us to keep both untarnished. Amen.

227   Living God, grant us true insight, understanding and wisdom and, though your way may seem foolish to some, teach us to walk it faithfully, to the glory of your name. Amen.

228   Living God, teach us the secret of true wisdom, in knowing and serving you, through Christ our Lord. Amen.

Hope and despair

see also Faithfulness of God; Guidance

229   Faithful God, when dreams are shattered and life seems devoid of meaning, speak afresh your word and assure us of your sovereign purpose, which will not be defeated, through Jesus Christ our Lord. Amen.

230   Gracious God, when the world seems bleak and all seems lost, remind us that through the agony and desolation of the cross, you were supremely at work bringing light out of darkness, hope out of despair, good out of evil and life out of death. So help us to look to the future with faith and to face the present at peace. Amen.

231   Living God, when life is hard and sorrows are many, lead us safely through the valley of tears until the horizon opens, the clouds lift and the sun shines once more, by the grace of Christ. Amen.

232   Living God, though we may feel crushed beyond redemption, teach us that your love will always overcome. Amen.

233   Lord of all, when life seems dark, help us to put our trust in you. Inspire us with the knowledge that, where all seems hopeless, you are sometimes most powerfully at work – challenging, deepening and strengthening faith, equipping us for new avenues of service and opening the way to a richer experience of your love. In that assurance, lead us forward, through Jesus Christ our Lord. Amen.

234   Gracious God, when tears are our food day and night, and when our heart is breaking within us, assure us of your love, reach out with your comfort, and help us to know that joy will come again. Amen.

235   Living God, no matter how helpless or hopeless we may feel, teach us that with you by our side, all things are always less dreadful than they seem. Amen.

236   Loving God, when life is hard and days are dark, enfold us in your arms and surround us with your loving care, holding us close for all eternity. Amen.

237   Living God, in the unpredictability of this life, faced with the apparent fickleness of fate, teach us to trust completely in the sure and certain hope you have given in Christ, for his name's sake. Amen.

238   Living God, when life fails to measure up to our expectations, remind us of the hope we have in Christ, through which we can expect fulfilment beyond measure, by his grace. Amen.

Fear

239   Living God, like everyone else there is much we fear, your love not granting us immunity from the trials and tribulations of this troubled world. Give us strength to meet whatever we may face, confident that nothing can finally come between us and your love in Jesus Christ our Lord. Amen.

240   Eternal God, teach us that though we may let go of you, you will always hold fast to us; that though we feel you are distant, you are always near. In that assurance, may we live each day, through Jesus Christ our Lord. Amen.

241   Mighty God, teach us that, whatever we fear, your love is able to see us through it, for it is stronger than evil, stronger than death itself, enduring for all eternity. To you be the praise and glory. Amen.

242   Lord Jesus Christ, as you stilled the storm so calm the turmoil within us. Put our minds at rest and our spirits at peace, secure in the knowledge of your never-failing love. Amen.

Sorrow

243   Lord Jesus Christ, reach out into our broken lives, and bring joy where there is sorrow, healing where there is hurt, hope where there is despair and peace where there is turmoil. In your name we pray. Amen.

244   Gracious God, teach us to use the dark moments we have been through to your glory, comforting others with the comfort we have found in you and staying close to them in their need as you have so faithfully stayed close to us. In Jesus' name we pray. Amen.

245   Lord Jesus Christ, when there has been no one else to bear the pain or share the hurt, no one to lend an ear or offer a shoulder to lean on, you have been there, faithful and true, ready to lift us up and tend our wounds, to listen to our cry and hold us close. Loving Lord, teach us to be there for others in turn. Amen.

246   Living God, teach us that, though we cannot always see it, you are always with us, even in the darkest moments of life, sharing in our anguish, carrying in yourself the agony of creation and working for that day when all suffering shall be ended and evil be no more. In that assurance, give us strength to face each day, whatever it might bring. Amen.

Intercession

For national and world leaders

247   Sovereign God, hear our prayer for all those to whom you have entrusted positions of leadership and responsibility. Grant them wisdom in their decisions, courage to hold fast to what is right, integrity in their dealings and a genuine commitment to the good of all those they serve. Guide them to know and do your will, for your kingdom's sake. Amen.

For peace in the world

248   Lord Jesus Christ, you came as the Prince of peace to bring healing to the nations – to overcome hatred with love, evil with good and darkness with light. Teach us what that means in today's complex and troubled world, where tension and unrest continue to dominate, where violence and the threat of war are all too real, and where mistrust, intolerance and prejudice still hold sway. Grant wisdom to leaders of nations, to all whose decisions will shape the future of this world and, by your Spirit, break down the barriers that divide us and bring closer the day of your kingdom. In your name we ask it. Amen.

For the homeless and refugees

249   Lord Jesus Christ, you know what it is to have nowhere to lay your head. Hear then our prayer for those who are homeless, who live as refugees or who are forced to live in makeshift and inadequate housing. Support the work of all who campaign on their behalf and challenge the consciences of those in authority so that they may do all in their power to provide somewhere for everyone to call their home. Amen.

For those who are hungry or thirsty

250   Lord Jesus Christ, you have promised that those who hunger and thirst after righteousness will be filled, but we pray today for those who simply hunger for food and thirst for water. In our fractured world of rich and poor, haves and have-nots, create a yearning for change and a passion for justice, and may that begin in us, our willingness to share and identify with others marking us out as your people, to the glory of your name. Amen.

For the poor

251   Living God, respond to the cry of the poor and the entreaties of the needy, and grant that the time will come when people everywhere receive a fair reward for their labours sufficient for all their needs; a time when this world's resources will be distributed justly, all having enough and none too much. Amen.

For all in need

252   Lord of all, hear the cry of the oppressed and exploited, the hungry and homeless, the sick and suffering, and help us to hear it too and to respond in your name. Amen.

253   God of grace, in the darkness of hatred, evil, sorrow and suffering may your light shine, this and every day. Amen.

For the sick

254   Lord Jesus Christ, as you touched those with leprosy, restored sight to the blind, brought peace to the disturbed and enabled the lame to walk, come now to all who are sick in body, mind and spirit, bringing again your healing touch and renewing grace. Amen.

For the less able

255   Living God, when limitations or disabilities make life hard, teach us that you love and value us, not for what we do, but for who we are, and may that knowledge teach us to appreciate and respect the worth of everyone we meet. Amen.

For the dying

256   Eternal God, we pray for those faced by the prospect of death, whether wrestling with terminal illness or coming to terms with failing health and advancing years. In all the fear and sorrow they may feel, give the assurance that not even death itself can separate them from your love and that you hold in store for them things more wonderful than they have yet begun to imagine, through Jesus Christ our Lord. Amen.

For the medical and caring professions

257   Lord Jesus Christ, as you reached out to the sick and suffering throughout your earthly ministry, bringing wholeness and healing to so many, reach out now through all who minister to body, mind and spirit, and through them grant your renewing, restoring touch. Amen.

For those facing sorrow

258   Lord Jesus Christ, friend of the friendless, hope of the hopeless and joy of the joyless, reach out into the hurt and pain of our world, the injustice, hunger and hatred, and may the seeds of your kingdom take root and grow. In all this world's sorrow and suffering, bring a harvest of justice and peace, love and celebration, for your name's sake. Amen.

259   Sovereign God, strength of the weak, hope of the despairing, comfort of the sorrowful, restorer of the broken, send us out renewed by your grace and help us to do all in our power to bring your transforming touch to others, through the healing power of our Lord Jesus Christ. Amen.

For the lonely

260   Lord Jesus Christ, may all those who feel isolated and unloved find in you a friend they can depend on and, through realising how much you value them, may they discover a sense of worth that leads to and informs their relationships with others. Amen.

Joyful response

see also Thanksgiving

261   Sovereign God, for the rich promise of each day, so full of possibilities, so awash with potential, and for the still greater anticipation of the life to come stretching out into eternity, we lift up our hearts in grateful worship and heartfelt praise. Amen.

262   Living God, for the joy of life, the joy of faith, the joy of knowing you, we give you our grateful praise. Amen.

263   Lord of all, may joy bubble up within us like a living spring, a bubbling brook, a gushing stream, a mighty river, flowing out to all we meet and carrying them along on the tide of your love, in jubilant celebration, through Jesus Christ our Lord. Amen.

264   Loving God, you have given us news of great joy – teach us to celebrate that truth each day. Amen.

265   Gracious God, you have given us good news for all the world, glad tidings beyond imagining: forgive us that so often we fail to reflect that in our lives. Teach us to live each day in a spirit of spontaneous rejoicing that testifies, in a way words can scarcely begin to express, to the matchless love and awesome gift of Christ our Lord. Amen.

266   Living God, you gave yourself wholly to us in Christ, glad to call us your children. Teach us to give ourselves similarly to you, proud to call you our Father and happy to be identified with your Son. In his name we ask it. Amen.

267   Gracious God, teach us to celebrate the innumerable blessings you shower upon us each day, and teach us also to recognise that this world offers only a foretaste of the riches you hold in store. Teach us to celebrate all we have received, but to set our hearts first on your kingdom and to show our gratitude for all your many gifts by offering back our lives in your service, to the glory of your name. Amen.

268   Loving Lord, we have celebrated the wonder of your grace, the breadth of your goodness and the awesome greatness of your purpose: so now we go on our way, our hearts singing within us, knowing that, as you have blessed us, so you will continue to shower us with your love, this and every day. Receive our praise. Amen.

269   Loving God, you gave without counting the cost, your sole desire to share your love and impart your joy: help us to give back to you, not as a duty or an afterthought, but as a joyful privilege, a giving of our best, an offering from the heart. Take what we are and consecrate it to your service, in the name of Christ. Amen.

270   Living God, teach us to give as gladly, as lovingly and as un-reservedly to you as you have given to us. Amen.

271   Gracious God, may the joy with which you have flooded our hearts flow freely from us, bringing joy to others in turn, to the glory of your name. Amen.

272   Living God, teach us that your love will never let us go, and so help us to make our response and bring our lives to you in joyful homage, knowing that you will continue to lead us until our journey's end, through Jesus Christ our Lord. Amen.

Laughter

273   Loving God, in all the serious business of life, with its pathos and difficulties, trials and tragedies, help us to see also the humorous side and to laugh even through the tears. Amen.

274   Lord of all, teach us never to laugh *at* others, but, when appropriate, to laugh *with* them, joyfully celebrating your gift of life in all its richness. Amen.

275   Gracious Lord, send us out with laughter in our eyes, a smile on our lips, a song in our heart and merriment in our soul, and so may we share the joy that you have given us, to the glory of your name. Amen.

276   Sovereign God, teach us that there is a time to grieve and a time to laugh, a time to be serious and a time to celebrate, a time for solemnity and a time for fun. Help us to know the difference. Amen.

Kingdom of God

277   Lord Jesus Christ, give us a vision of your kingdom and show us the part you would have us play in bringing it closer. Help us to strive each day towards that goal, for your name's sake. Amen.

278   Loving God, help us to see around us the seeds of your kingdom, and to nurture them lovingly until that day dawns when your will is done and you are all in all. Amen.

279   Loving God, when we pray 'Your kingdom come, your will be done', teach us to mean it, however hard working towards its fulfilment may be. Amen.

280   Sovereign God, we have asked it so many times before, but we ask it again, together with all your people: 'Your kingdom come, your will be done, on earth as it is in heaven.' Amen.

281   Living God, give us faith and courage to live out the foolishness of the gospel, following the way of humility, service and self-sacrifice, and so may we bring your kingdom closer here on earth. Amen.

282   The seed is sown, the kingdom is growing, the harvest will come. Loving God, we praise you for that knowledge, and we offer you now our love, our faith and our service, in the name of Christ. Amen.

Light in our darkness

283 God of life, may the promise of the sunrise be echoed in our minds, the warmth of the midday sun flow into our hearts and the peace of the sunset touch our souls, and, when life seems dark, teach us to remember that still you are with us and that we will again see your light. Amen.

284 Eternal God, when life seems a puzzle and faith itself can make no sense of it, lead us forward out of darkness into light, out of confusion into certainty, out of the storm into tranquillity. Put our minds at rest and our spirits at peace, through Jesus Christ our Lord. Amen.

285 The night is turning to day, darkness is turning to light – it is time to wake from our sleep. Wherever there is sorrow, fear, need or hurt, let us reach out in the name of Christ and may his joy and peace, healing and compassion, dawn through us, until morning has broken and the day of his kingdom is here. Amen.

286 God of light, be with us in our darkness, until night passes and your light breaks through. Amen.

287 Gracious God, even when all seems dark, teach us that your light will always shine through. Amen.

288 Lord Jesus Christ, may the flame of faith burn brightly within us, and your light shine in our hearts, so that we, in turn, may bring light to others, to the glory of your name. Amen.

Lord's Supper

Preparing to receive

289   Lord Jesus Christ, we remember again at this table that you didn't just talk about love but supremely demonstrated it on the cross, enduring sorrow, suffering and death to bring us life. Forgive us our lack of love for you and others, our inability to translate words into actions, and help us to live more fully as your people, to the glory of your name. Amen.

290   Lord Jesus Christ, we are here not only to remember what you once did but also to celebrate what you continue to do, not just to recall the past but also to anticipate the future, not simply to acknowledge your death but also to affirm your risen life and to celebrate the new life you have given us in turn. Help us to live it to your glory, for your name's sake. Amen.

291   Lord of the cross, the empty tomb and your Church in this and every age, through bread and wine, we meet and greet you. Amen.

292   Lord Jesus Christ, we have so much to celebrate, our lives overwhelmed with good things, yet without you we are empty. By your grace, fill us. You flood each day with your blessings, too many to number, but our souls without you are parched. Come to us again and quench our inner thirst. Meet us here and nourish us with the bread of life. Touch our hearts and refresh us with streams of living water. Amen.

293   Gracious God, we know we have no right to be here, no claim on your love and no reason to expect your goodness, but we come at your gracious invitation, trusting in your mercy and seeking forgiveness for all our faults. For the welcome you so freely give us in Christ, receive our thanks and praise, in his name. Amen.

294　Lord Jesus Christ, we remember that you broke bread and shared wine with those who, in different ways, would fail you, none more so than Peter, who, for all his protestations of loyalty, would deny you three times. We thank you for the great truth that this speaks of: your willingness to accept us as we are, your love that goes on loving despite our many faults and failings, your grace that goes beyond any deserving. So now we eat and drink in joyful worship and grateful praise. Amen.

295　Lord Jesus Christ, as we eat and drink together, help us not just to remember but also to honour you, celebrating your gift of new life and committing ourselves afresh to your service. Amen.

After communion

296　Lord Jesus Christ, we thank you that, though we are many, each having our own experience of life and own experience of your love, yet we are one, called to be your body, your people, your Church. For overcoming all that keeps us from you and one another, receive our praise. Amen.

297　Lord Jesus Christ, continue to feed us each day, not just through bread and wine but also through your living word, your life-giving Spirit and your daily presence. Fill the hunger within us so that we shall be truly satisfied. Amen.

298　Lord Jesus Christ, we have remembered your death, we have celebrated your resurrection, we have rejoiced in the wonder of your love. Send us out now to proclaim the good news so that others will know you died for them and in turn celebrate the new life you offer and the love you so freely give. Amen.

299　Lord Jesus Christ, we thank you that you have satisfied our hunger and our thirst with living bread and new wine. Go with us now and help us to share what we have received, so that those we meet may glimpse a little of your love and, through coming to know you, find nourishment for their souls. Amen.

300   Lord Jesus Christ, you tell us to break bread and share wine until you come. Send us out then to prepare your way, to work for your kingdom and to do all we can to bring that day of your coming nearer. Amen.

301   The bread has been broken, the wine poured out. The supper is over and the world still waits. Let us go then and offer our service, our faith and our love, until the world rejoices and the kingdom is come. Amen.

302   Lord Jesus Christ, as your blood was poured out for many, help us to pour ourselves out in your service; to give freely back to you who gave everything for us. Amen.

303   We have come in faith; now let us go in peace. We have received from the Lord's hand; now let us give to others in his name. We have eaten bread and drunk wine; now let us go and share his love. We have proclaimed the Lord's death; now let us go and make known his life. The supper is ended but the journey continues. Let us go with confidence, for the Lord is with us, now and always. Amen.

Love

God's love of us

304   Gracious God, we go on our way knowing that your love is all in all, now and for evermore. Amen.

305   Gracious God, we thank you for loving us before we ever loved you, and for continuing to love us even when we find it hard to love ourselves. Teach us to accept what we are and so to grow into what we can become. Amen.

306   Living God, may your love flow to us, reaching down to bless and within to bring joy. May your love flow through us, reaching upwards in worship and outwards in service. May *your* love kindle *our* love, to the glory of your name. Amen.

307   Lord Jesus Christ, help us to look to you who showed us love in action – a love that stays true, trusts, hopes and perseveres in all things – and help us truly to realise that, without such love, all our words, faith and religion count for nothing. Amen.

308   Lord Jesus, we bring all we are before you – the bad as well as the good, the doubt as well as the faith, the sorrow as well as the joy, the despair as well as the hope – knowing that you love us so much that you died for us despite it all. Receive our praise. Amen.

Our love of God

309   Gracious God, so dwell within us that we will rejoice each day at all your mercies and love you with heart and soul and mind. Amen.

310   Gracious God, take our love for you and fan it into a mighty flame so that we may love you as you deserve, to the glory of your name. Amen.

311   Lord Jesus Christ, live in our hearts, fill our souls, renew our minds, so that we may know and love you fully, just as you know and love us. Amen.

312   Sovereign God, teach us what it means to love you with body, mind and soul, and help us to be as committed to you as you are to us, through Jesus Christ our Lord. Amen.

313   Lord Jesus Christ, teach us to love as you love, and to offer you the devotion you deserve and that you so freely show to all. Amen.

Openness to God's love

314   God of all, break through the barriers that shut our minds fast, and help us to see things both as they really are and as you can help them become. Move within us, in the name of Christ. Amen.

315   Gracious God, help us to open our lives to your searching gaze and our hearts to your redeeming love. Amen.

316   Gracious God, teach us that before we can give anything, we need first to receive, and so open our lives to your saving, renewing love, through Christ our Lord. Amen.

317   Lord Jesus Christ, show us those areas of our lives that are closed to your love, and help us to open them fully to you, so that you may live in us and work through us, to the glory of your name. Amen.

Loving others

318   Gracious God, give us courage, faith and humility to let go of hatred and to follow the way of love, through Jesus Christ our Lord. Amen.

319   Gracious God, take the little love we have, nurture, deepen, and expand it, until we have learned what love really means, until your love flows through our hearts, until love is all in all. Amen.

320   Gracious God, teach us the secret of a love that goes on loving, despite all it faces. Amen.

321   Lord Jesus Christ, come to us, live in us, love through us. Amen.

322   Lord Jesus Christ, you know what it is to give, for you gave your all. Teach us that whatever we give, we shall receive far more, and so use us to show your love and bring your blessing to others, to the glory of your name. Amen.

323   Lord Jesus Christ, you tell us that the whole law is summed up in the command to love: help us to understand what that means, so that this truth may shape our decisions, our attitudes and our life, to your glory. Amen.

324   Gracious God, for your gracious love that no one deserves yet all can receive, we give you our praise. Teach us to love in turn, through Jesus Christ our Lord. Amen.

Morning

see also New beginnings; Worship: Approach

325   Living God, open our hearts to the possibilities of this new day – to everything it has to offer and, above all, to all the ways you will be at work within it. Help us to know and recognise your living presence at every moment, and so to live constantly seeking your will and glory, through Jesus Christ our Lord. Amen.

326   Creator God, whatever the person we may have been, help us today to glimpse the person we can be and, by your grace, shall become, through Jesus Christ our Lord. Amen.

327   Sovereign God, teach us to live this and every day focusing not on what *we* can't do, but on what *you* can. Amen.

328   God of grace, as dawn has broken once more, so may the light of your love dawn afresh in our hearts and shine out of our lives, to the glory of your name. Amen.

329   Gracious God, despite our good intentions we know that we will fail you again today, as we have failed you so many times before – our faith frail and our commitment weak. Thank you for the knowledge that you will not fail us, come what may – your purpose strong and your love stronger than words can tell. May that assurance sustain and inspire us, this and every day. Amen.

330   Sovereign God, teach us to live this day to the full by living it not just for ourselves but also, and above all, for you. Amen.

331   Living God, show us this day what you would have us do, where you would have us go, what you would have us say and how you would have us serve. In the name of Christ we ask it. Amen.

332   Gracious God, help us to greet each day as your gift, to spend each day in your service, to rejoice each day in your love and to live each day for your glory, through Jesus Christ our Lord. Amen.

333   Merciful God, as we begin this new day, help us to let go of the past and trust you for the future. So may we celebrate the present, rejoicing in the fullness of life you so graciously bestow upon us. Amen.

334   Loving God, teach us this day to look beyond the obvious and immediate, and to live each moment in the light of your sovereign grace, through which you are able to do far more than we can ever ask or imagine, through Jesus Christ our Lord. Amen.

New beginnings

see also Morning

335   Gracious God, help us to face the flaws everyone knows about, and those we try to hide even from ourselves, knowing that your nature is always to have mercy and to help us start again. Take us and make us new, for Christ's sake. Amen.

336   Gracious God, take what we can never change, and, by your grace, make it new. Amen.

337   Lord Jesus Christ, teach us that new life does not begin in the distant future but here and now, and so may we receive your gracious gift with glad thanksgiving. Amen.

338   Loving God, teach us what it means to be made new, and help us to receive each moment as a fresh start, through the grace of Christ. Amen.

339   Sovereign God, open our eyes to your continuing purpose and renewing power, and so help us to see each apparent conclusion as the start of a fresh chapter in life. Amen.

340   Living God, from the unpromising material of our lives, fashion your new creation, through Jesus Christ our Lord. Amen.

341   Lord Jesus Christ, move within us and draw us closer to you, so that the newness of this day may be echoed in newness of life springing fresh within us every day, now and always. Amen.

Offering

see also Joyful response; Self-denial and sacrifice; Thanksgiving

342   Sovereign God, help us to give you not just our money but also our love, our time and our service, each offered to you as a sign of our faith and in response to your goodness, through Jesus Christ our Lord. Amen.

343   Living God, take what we give, what we are and what we long to be, and use all to foster your kingdom here on earth. Amen.

344   Lord Jesus Christ, who gave so much so freely, work within us, who give so little so grudgingly. Help us to sacrifice something of our riches for you, remembering that you surrendered all for us. Amen.

345   Lord Jesus Christ, when we give to you, teach us to think not of what we can afford but of what you deserve. Amen.

346   Living God, take our bodies and let them work for you, take our minds and let them dream for you, take our hearts and let them beat for you, take our spirits and let them soar for you, through Jesus Christ our Lord. Amen.

347   Lord Jesus Christ, whatever we give to you is as nothing compared to what you have given to us. Receive our praise and accept our thanks. Amen.

Peace

see also Intercession: For peace in the world; Stillness and reflection

Peacemaking

348   Lord Jesus Christ, teach us not just to be *at* peace but also to work *for* peace, to the glory of your name. Amen.

349   Lord of all, open our hearts to others through being open to you, and help us to pursue all that makes for peace until that day when you come in Christ to establish your kingdom and make all things new. In his name we pray. Amen.

Peace of God

350   Lord Jesus Christ, when we find ourselves overwhelmed by life's problems and struggling to stay afloat, be there to still the storm and to grant your peace. Amen.

351   Lord Jesus Christ, give us grace to see the point of view of others, humility to accept when we are wrong and sensitivity in our attitude when we are right, so that we may live as peacemakers, for your name's sake. Amen.

352   Gracious God, teach us to live each day in the light of the incredible yet wonderful truth that you love us completely and want us to be at peace with ourselves and with you. In Christ's name we ask it. Amen.

353   Lord Jesus Christ, speak your word and calm the troubled waters of our lives, the turmoil of mind and restlessness of spirit, granting the peace that you alone can give. In your name we ask it. Amen.

Praise

see also Faithfulness of God; Worship

354   Sovereign God, we can hardly begin to comprehend your power, barely grasp the extent of your love and scarcely start to fathom the awesome breadth of your purpose: we glimpse only a little of the truth, yet that little causes us to gasp in wonder and kneel in homage. Receive our praise, for we offer it in humble and reverent worship, through Jesus Christ our Lord. Amen.

355   Gracious God, who shared our humanity from birth to death so that we might share your eternity, receive our grateful praise, through Jesus Christ our Lord. Amen.

356   Living God, for the knowledge that, whatever this life may bring, you hold new life in store, we give you our thanks and praise. Amen.

357   Lord Jesus Christ, meet with us afresh each day, and open our eyes to see you, our ears to hear you, our minds to know you and our hearts to love you. So may we glimpse a little more of your glory and our lives sing your praises in joyful worship. Amen.

358   Sovereign God, your greatness fills the heavens, your power sustains the universe, your love supports all creation and your purpose extends to all times and all people, yet you have time for the very least of us – time for all! For that most awesome of truths, we give you our praise. Amen.

359   Almighty God, yours is the hand that created the universe, the power that shapes the course of history, the love that moves through all things and the grace that opens up the way to life, yet all that is merely a fraction of your greatness. Receive our praise, and open our hearts to know you better each day, until that great day when we meet you face to face and rejoice in the wonder of your presence, through the grace of Christ. Amen.

360   Living God, remind us that, though you are far above all human thought, you are always near, made known through Christ and dwelling within us through your Holy Spirit. Receive our grateful praise. Amen.

361   Mighty God, though we stretch imagination to the limit, we barely begin to glimpse how wonderful you are. Though you sometimes seem distant, you are ever near. Whatever we face, wherever we are, you are there, seen or unseen, your hand always at work. For the constancy of your love and the faithfulness of your purpose, we give you our praise, in the name of Christ. Amen.

362   Sovereign God, we cannot praise you too much. Forgive us that we fail to praise you enough. Amen.

363   Almighty God, open our eyes afresh to your greatness, your power and your sovereignty over all. Give us again a glimpse of your glory, not just here but everywhere, not just today but every day, so that our hearts may be overwhelmed by your splendour and our souls may soar in exultation, and in joyful, reverent praise. Amen.

Acclamations of praise

364   Living God, for your greatness beyond imagining, your grace beyond deserving, your goodness beyond measuring and your love beyond comparing, we give you our praise in awe and wonder. Amen.

365   Living God, you have given us joy that knows no bounds, mercy beyond all our deserving, hope that can never be exhausted, peace that passes understanding and love that exceeds anything we can ever ask or think of. To you be glory, praise and honour, now and always. Amen.

366   Sovereign God, for your blessings too many to number, and your goodness too wonderful for words, we give you our praise. Amen.

367   To God who is higher than our highest thoughts, yet closer than our closest friend, be thanks and praise, glory and honour, this day and for evermore. Amen.

368   To you, O God, be praise and glory, worship and adoration, today and always. Amen.

369   Gracious God, you bless us beyond our imagining, love us beyond our dreaming, forgive us beyond our deserving and use us beyond our hoping. To you be praise and thanksgiving, honour and adoration, now and always. Amen.

370   Living God, for your love beyond price and your goodness beyond measure, receive our praise, in the name of Christ. Amen.

371   Lord Jesus Christ, our Saviour, able to keep our foot from slipping and to present us faultless and brimming over with joy into the glorious presence of God, to you be glory and majesty, dominion and power, now and for evermore. Amen. *(Adapted from Jude 24)*

372   Sovereign God, for opening through Christ the way to know and love you, receive our praise. Amen.

373   To God who is always forgiving, always loving, always offering a new beginning, be honour and glory, praise and thanksgiving, this day and for ever. Amen.

374   To the one whose goodness is without equal, whose love is beyond comparison, whose mercy is beyond understanding and whose power is beyond words be praise and glory, worship and thanksgiving, now and always. Amen.

Prayer, wrestling in

375   Lord Jesus Christ, when we cannot or do not say the things we mean to, speak for us, through your Spirit, in the presence of God. Amen.

376   Sovereign God, teach us not only how to pray but how to help make our prayers become reality. Teach us to be your hands and feet, your lips and ears, the agents of your purpose, and so work through us to the glory of your name. Amen.

377   Lord, we bring ourselves, not as we would like to be, nor as we know we should be, but as we are. Hear us as we pour out our souls to you, and answer us through your grace. Amen.

378   Living God, give us faith to persevere in prayer, courage to trust in your promises, and humility to recognise that your answer will come in your own time and your own way. Amen.

379   Loving God, although we talk much about prayer, we are weak when it comes to praying and weaker still in turning prayers into action. Forgive us our neglect of prayer, our reluctance to take it seriously, our failure to devote time to you. Forgive us our empty or half-hearted prayers, offered more out of duty or habit than serious intent. Teach us how to wrestle in prayer and to act upon our words, and so may we truly pray to your glory, in the name of Christ. Amen.

380   Living God, give us the faith we need to pray, and teach us to pray to you in faith. Amen.

381   Lord Jesus Christ, like your disciples long ago, our prayer today is simply 'Teach us how to pray'. Amen.

382   Loving God, teach us when we need to keep on praying, and when we should let go, and help us to know the difference. Amen.

383   Gracious God, we thank you for all the prayers you have answered over the years, and we bring you those that seem unanswered, knowing that you are always ready to hear us and that you always, finally, answer. Receive our praise, through Jesus Christ our Lord. Amen.

384   Living God, when you do not seem to answer, help us to listen harder, and when you *do* speak, teach us to listen and respond; through Jesus Christ our Lord. Amen.

Presence of God

385   Go out into the world rejoicing, for God is waiting to meet you and surprise you with the beauty of his presence: in the song of a blackbird, the hooting of an owl, the cry of a fox; in the opening of a bud, the fragrance of a flower, the falling of a leaf; in the murmur of the breeze, the rushing of the wind, the howling of the gale; in the babbling of the brook, the rippling of the stream, the crashing of the waves; in the peace of the meadows, the freedom of the hills, the grandeur of the mountains; in the cry of a baby, the laughter of children, the hum of conversation; in the pat on the shoulder, the handshake of welcome, the embrace of a loved one; in the noise of the factory, the routine of the office, the bustle of the shop. God is here, God is there, God is everywhere. Go then, and walk with him, in the light of his love, and the fullness of life. Amen.

386   Gracious God, open our eyes to your presence and, just as you walk with us, help us to walk with you. Amen.

387   Living God, we thank you that you are not just with us here in prayer but also in the daily round of life, waiting to meet us, lead us and bless us. Help us to glimpse your presence, and to live each moment conscious that you are by our side, to your praise and glory. Amen.

388   Lord Jesus Christ, when we seek God but do not find him, help us to look to you and so recognise that, seen or unseen, he is at work, fulfilling his sovereign purpose. In your name we pray. Amen.

389   Sovereign God, open our soul to your living presence, so we may glimpse your glory and discover the sacredness of every moment. Amen.

390   Sovereign God, when we cannot discern your hand or sense your presence, help us to understand that you are no less near than you have ever been, and that, seen or unseen, you continue to work out your purpose. Amen.

Questions of faith

391   Almighty God, when faith is a puzzle and we look in vain for answers, teach us when to keep on searching and when we must learn to live with mystery. Amen.

392   Sovereign God, give us humility to acknowledge our weakness beside your greatness, faith to trust in you despite our doubts, joy in knowing you despite the limitations of our understanding, and peace in serving you despite our fears as to what you might ask. In Jesus' name. Amen.

393   Sovereign God, save us from a faith that asks no questions, and from a faith that asks too many, through Jesus Christ, our Lord. Amen.

394   Gracious God, give us courage to ask questions, faith to live with them, and grace to grow through them, to the glory of your name. Amen.

395   Living God, give us wisdom to know when we need to question, to search for greater understanding, deeper awareness and a fuller knowledge of your love, but help us also to recognise when questions are misplaced, saying more about us than you, obscuring rather than revealing, destroying rather than building up our faith. Amen.

396   Lord of all, teach us that, though we might ask all the right questions, we can never find all the right answers, for you are above all, over all and beyond all. Teach us to keep that sense of perspective, through Jesus Christ our Lord. Amen.

397   Gracious God, when we cannot find the answers we seek, teach us to leave all things in your hands, trusting for tomorrow through what we know of you today. Amen.

398   Sovereign God, teach us to base our faith not on what *might be* but on what *has been* and what *is*. May all you have done and continue to do inspire us to trust in the future you hold for us, confident that, as you are with us now, so you shall be by our side for all eternity, through Jesus Christ our Lord. Amen.

399 Loving God, we come to you today, offering not only our faith but also our doubt, praying that you will use both to lead us closer to you. Amen.

400 Mighty and mysterious God, when we cannot make sense of the jigsaw of our lives, remind us that now we see only in part, but one day we will see you face to face and know you even as we are fully known. Amen.

401 Sovereign God, in the puzzles and mysteries of life, and in all that seems to contradict our faith, help us to believe still that you are there and that your purpose will not be defeated. Amen.

402 Almighty God, open our eyes afresh to your greatness and remind us again that your ways are not *our* ways nor your thoughts *our* thoughts. So may we glimpse once more your glory, and, though we do not always understand, may we walk in faith, in Jesus' name. Amen.

403 Good Lord, from thinking we have all the answers, and from thinking too much of questions, deliver us, in the name of Christ. Amen.

404 Lord of all, give us sufficient trust to acknowledge our questions openly and to offer them honestly to you in prayer, confident that they are a part of faith, able to lead us to new insights and a deeper understanding of your purpose, through Jesus Christ our Lord. Amen.

Relationships

see also Love: Loving others; Worth of all

Being honest

405   Loving God, grant us grace to be honest with you, with others and with ourselves. Amen.

Encouraging

406   As you encourage us in so many ways, so may we encourage others in turn, through Jesus Christ our Lord. Amen.

Expressing appreciation

407   Loving God, teach us not just to thank *you* but to thank all who in any way enrich our lives. Help us, through word and deed, to show our appreciation of everything they do and everything they mean. Amen.

Integrity and sensitivity

408   Living God, teach us what it means to be true to ourselves, faithful to you yet sensitive to others, through Jesus Christ our Lord. Amen.

Judging

409   Living God, before we jump to conclusions and pass judgement on others, help us to look again, and with your help to look deeper, recognising that you alone can judge the heart. In Christ's name, we pray. Amen.

Loving others

410   Gracious God, teach us to forgive as you have forgiven, to care as you care for us, and to love as you love all, through Jesus Christ our Lord. Amen.

411   Gracious God, in all our dealings give us a listening ear, an open mind, a caring spirit and a warm heart, through Jesus Christ our Lord. Amen.

Openness

412   Living God, help us to open our lives to you by opening them first to others, through Jesus Christ our Lord. Amen.

Self-denial and sacrifice

see also Offering; Serving others

413 Gracious God, you became poor so that we might become rich: help us to become a little poorer so that we might discover true riches. Amen.

414 Lord Jesus Christ, as you put us first, surrendering your life for our sake, help us to put you first in return. Amen.

415 Lord Jesus Christ, help us to use our possessions in your service rather than allowing them to possess us. Amen.

416 Lord Jesus Christ, teach us the values of your kingdom and the joy of knowing you, so that we may put you first and self second, to the glory of your name. Amen.

417 Lord Jesus Christ, teach us to let go of self, to focus on the things that really matter, and so discover life in all its fullness, through your grace. Amen.

418 God of justice, quicken our consciences and stir our hearts so that we may show our faith not simply in easy words but in costly actions. Teach us what it means to deny ourselves and, in doing so, may we bring joy, help and hope to others. Amen.

Serving others

see also Self-denial and sacrifice

419   Gracious God, help us to see with your eyes, to reach out with your touch, to love with your heart, and to respond always with your gentleness. Amen.

420   Lord Jesus Christ, teach us not to serve ourselves but others, not to seek our own ends but your will, and so may all we are and all we do bring glory to your name. Amen.

421   Living God, teach us that this small world is *your* world, and so show us where, in responding to others, we can respond to you. Amen.

422   Lord Jesus Christ, you call us, as you called your first disciples, to follow you: not simply to believe, declare our faith and confess you as Lord, but to keep on following wherever you lead. Help us to do that faithfully, pursuing the way of love and accepting the road of sacrifice. Amen.

423   Living God, teach us that we need others just as they need us, and so may we discharge our responsibilities faithfully within the great company of your people, to the glory of your name. Amen.

424   Living God, we have come to you seeking your word and guidance. Now help us to go for you, in joyful service, to work for your kingdom, share your love and make known the gospel. Amen.

425   Living God, whatever you call us to do, help us to perform it faithfully, gladly and wholeheartedly, to the glory of your name. Amen.

426   Lord Jesus Christ, as you are always thinking of us, reaching out in love, so teach us to reach out to others, for your name's sake. Amen.

427   Lord Jesus Christ, as you have affirmed life for us, so may we affirm it for all in word and deed, to the glory of your name. Amen.

428   Lord Jesus Christ, as you have been there for us, help us to be there for others, for your name's sake. Amen.

429   Lord Jesus Christ, friend of the friendless, reach out to us and help us to reach out in turn, through your grace. Amen.

430   Lord Jesus Christ, teach us that a little in your hands can achieve more than a fortune in ours, and so inspire us to give generously in your service, to the glory of your name. Amen.

431   Lord Jesus Christ, teach us to serve you, not for any recognition we might receive, but for the joy of contributing to your kingdom. Amen.

432   Lord Jesus Christ, who became poor for our sake, teach us, having so much, to remember the many who have so little and, in responding to them, may we respond to you. Amen.

433   Lord Jesus Christ, you bore our sins on the cross, carrying there the burdens of all. Teach us to bear the burdens of others, in your name. Amen.

434   Lord Jesus Christ, you did not just go the extra mile – you gave everything, enduring death on a cross so that we might live. Work within us and help us to be willing to give of ourselves in the service of others, for your name's sake. Amen.

435   Lord of all, may our worship of you be reflected in a commitment to others and a passion for justice. Amen.

436   Lord Jesus Christ, teach us that in serving others we are also serving you. Amen.

437   Sovereign God, teach us to hear your voice in the cry of the poor, hungry, sick and oppressed, and teach us, in responding to them, to respond to you. Amen.

Stillness and reflection

see also Peace: Peace of God

438   Teach us, Lord, to take stock, thoughtfully, honestly and prayerfully, so that we may see ourselves as we really are rather than as we imagine ourselves to be. Amen.

439   Gracious God, teach us not to walk unthinkingly through life but to reflect on all we see and experience, and thus glimpse your hand at work. Amen.

440   Living God, whatever the pressures and duties of the day, teach us to find time for stillness, and, in seeing you there, may we see you always and everywhere, through the grace of Christ. Amen.

441   Lord of all, we have made time and space for quietness to hear your voice. Go with us now into the turmoil of life, with all its noise and confusion, all its demands and responsibilities, and may your peace rest with us there, this day and for evermore. Amen.

442   Sovereign God, in the rush and bustle of life, teach us to recognise the one thing worth pursuing above all else – your awesome love revealed in Christ. Amen.

443   God of the still small voice, teach us each day to find time for moments of quietness – time to ponder, to pray and to meditate on your gracious love. Breathe peace within our souls, so that we may see the demands and responsibilities of daily life in a fresh light, able to meet them with rekindled faith and calm assurance, through Jesus Christ our Lord. Amen.

444   Gentle and gracious God, calm our minds where they are troubled, ease our bodies where they are weary, soothe our spirits where they are in turmoil. Teach us to find our strength in stillness and quiet and, in the love of Christ, to find rest for our souls. Amen.

Strength in weakness

445   Jesus Christ, crucified Lord and servant king, take our weakness and our frailty and, by your grace, use us to achieve great things for your kingdom. Amen.

446   Living God, help us not to look at what we are, nor at what we can do, but rather at what you can achieve within us by your grace, through Jesus Christ our Lord. Amen.

447   Living God, teach us that you can do more with a little than we could hope to achieve had we the whole world at our disposal. Amen.

448   Living God, though we can do nothing, teach us that you can do everything, through Jesus Christ, our Lord. Amen.

449   Sovereign God, teach us to look not at our weakness but at your power, through Jesus Christ our Lord. Amen.

450   Sovereign God, teach us to let go of our fears and to trust in your strength, this day and always. Amen.

451   Lord Jesus Christ, we go in your strength, knowing that, whatever we may face, you will be sufficient for all our needs. In you we put our trust, now and always. Amen.

Thanksgiving

see also Joyful response; Offering

452   Gracious God, however often we thank you, we can never thank you enough, for your blessings are too many to number and your goodness is too wonderful for words. So we come, as we have come so often before, to express our gratitude for all we have received from your bountiful hands. Amen.

453   Living God, for the times we have forgotten to say thank you, and the times we have expressed gratitude but not really meant it, forgive us. Receive now our grateful and heartfelt acknowledgement for the countless good things you have showered upon us. Amen.

454   Gracious God, help us not only to ask in faith but also to receive with gratitude, through Jesus Christ our Lord. Amen.

455   Loving God, teach us to celebrate all we have received, but to set our heart first on your kingdom and to show our gratitude for all your gifts by offering back our lives in your service, to the glory of your name. Amen.

456   Living God, help us not just to express thankfulness but also to show it in the most eloquent way possible: through joyfully receiving your gracious gifts and faithfully using them to serve your will and bring you glory. Amen.

457   Gracious God, teach us to celebrate and savour every moment of every day with heartfelt praise and joyful thanksgiving, now and always. Amen.

458   Living God, we thank you that, however great we think you are, we have scarcely begun to understand the fullness of your gift in Christ. Amen.

459   Gracious God, instead of coveting the things we do not have, help us to appreciate and give thanks for the treasures we do have. Amen.

460   Lord Jesus Christ, we offer you our lives, not to settle a debt or buy your favour but as an expression of our love, a token of our gratitude, an outpouring of our worship and a symbol of our commitment. Accept us, and use us in your service, for your name's sake. Amen.

461   Living God, for the simple yet wonderful message that in Christ you lived and died among us, and that in him you defeated death, rising again so that we might live, we thank you, in his name. Amen.

Time

see also Faithfulness of God: Yesterday, today, for ever

Committing time to God

462   Gracious God, take this moment, this minute, this hour, this day. Take our lives and use them for your kingdom, in the name of Christ. Amen.

463   Gracious God, teach us to recognise time as your gift, held in trust by your grace, and so help us to use it wisely, rather than squander a priceless treasure. In Christ's name we ask it. Amen.

464   Gracious God, we praise you for what has been, we thank you for what is, and we commit to you what shall be, in Jesus' name. Amen.

Using each moment

465   Eternal God, teach us to use each moment wisely, open to your guidance, so that we understand what is right for each occasion. Teach us to see time not as a threat but as your gift, and so may we live life to the full, as you desire. Amen.

466   Gracious God, teach us to take each moment as it comes and to live it to the full. Amen.

Living in the present

467   God of past, present and future, teach us to let go of our yesterdays, to trust in your tomorrow, and so to rejoice today, celebrating the fullness of life that you have given, through Jesus Christ our Lord. Amen.

468   Living God, teach us to remember the lessons of the past, so that we may appreciate the present and work always for a better future, in the name of Christ. Amen.

469   Lord Jesus Christ, save us from so dwelling on all that has been that we overlook your blessings now and your promise of joy to come. Amen.

470   Lord Jesus Christ, teach us to remember, teach us to look forward in faith, and so teach us to live each moment in the light of your love. Amen.

Time for God and others

471   Living God, help us to find time for you, and so to find time for all. Amen.

472   Loving God, as you have time for us, help us to have time for others and for you. Amen.

God's timing

473   Living God, help us to recognise that what may seem the right time may be wrong, and what may seem the wrong time may be right. Teach us to seek your guidance, and to respond as you direct. Amen.

474   Sovereign God, when we start to fret over the loss of a single minute, remind us that your love will continue for all eternity. Amen.

Trust

see also Faithfulness of God

475   Eternal God, we put ourselves in your hands, knowing that your kingdom shall come and your will be done, through Jesus Christ our Lord. Amen.

476   Gracious God, help us to believe in you as much as you believe in us. Amen.

477   Gracious God, in the good and the bad, the happy and the sad, help us to keep on trusting you, confident that your purpose will win through and your love triumph over all. Amen.

478   Living God, teach us to trust in you, knowing that what we cannot do, you can! Amen.

479   Lord Jesus Christ, before we do anything else, help us always to turn to you, and so may we know your hand upon us, this and every day. Amen.

480   Lord Jesus Christ, open our eyes to all you have done and all you are doing, and so help us to glimpse all you are yet able to do by your sovereign grace. Amen.

481   Loving God, we do not know what lies ahead, except that there will be a mixture of good and bad, joy and sorrow, but we know for certain that, in life or in death, you will be with us, waiting to enrich our lives, bestow your blessing and fulfil your sovereign purpose. In that faith, we commit the future to you, through Jesus Christ our Lord. Amen.

482   Sovereign God, instead of seeing what *we* cannot do, teach us to see what *you* can, through Jesus Christ, our Lord and Saviour. Amen.

483   Sovereign God, teach us that though much is beyond *us*, nothing is beyond *you*. Amen.

484   Sovereign God, teach us to trust in you even when we cannot see the way ahead. Help us to walk in faith, even when faith seems foolish. Grant us grace to entrust ourselves to your everlasting arms, in the assurance that you will be sufficient for all our needs. Amen.

485   Living Lord, when you ask us to go out in your name – to listen to your voice, to venture into the unknown, to let go of self and to reach out in love – teach us to be strong, courageous, obedient and faithful; teach us to say 'yes'. Amen.

_____ Unity and division _____

486   Lord Jesus Christ, reach out in love to this foolish, faithless world and, by your grace, tend our wounds. Come again to all who are hurting and hating, and overcome the things that still keep us apart, for your name's sake. Amen.

487   Lord Jesus Christ, teach us that whatever might divide us from other Christians, far more unites us with them, and so may we be open to all, recognising the unity we share in you. Amen.

488   Gracious God, forgive us when differences drive us apart from others, and so fill us with the love of Christ that we may share a common and unbreakable bond with all your people, in the name of Christ. Amen.

489   Lord Jesus Christ, help us to see differences in others not as a threat but as an opportunity, and so help us to live in unity with all your people, to the glory of your name. Amen.

490   Lord Jesus Christ, may we not belong to you in name only, but be one with you and all your people, working together for your kingdom, to the glory of your name. Amen.

491   Lord of all, deliver us from a faith so rigid it is closed to new insights, from a vision so narrow it is closed to new horizons, from dogmas so rigid we are closed to your Spirit, and from convictions so fixed we are closed to other Christians. Open our eyes to you and to one another, in Jesus' name. Amen.

492   Sovereign God, save us from being so full of ourselves and preoccupied with our rightness that we have no time to learn from others. Deliver us from being so limited by our own horizons and parochial concerns that we have no time for you. Teach us that, if we would grow in faith, service and witness, we must first grow together, closer to you and all your people. Amen.

Wholeness and healing

see also Hope and despair: Sorrow

493   Sovereign God, take our fragmented lives and, through your gracious touch, make us whole. Take our broken world and, through your sovereign grace, bring healing. Reach out *to* us and *through* us, in the name of Christ. Amen.

494   Lord Jesus Christ, take the bruised, battered and broken pieces of our lives and, by your grace, put us together again. Amen.

495   Living God, teach us to bring our needs to you, knowing that, though you may not always respond as we want you to, you will always respond in love, providing for our needs, granting us peace and making us whole. In the name of Christ we ask it. Amen.

496   God of grace, breathe health into our bodies, love into our hearts, peace into our minds and joy into our spirits. Send us out now, made new, made whole, to live life fully as you desire. In Christ's name we ask it. Amen.

497   Lord Jesus Christ, touch the raw spots in our lives, the aching places deep within, and bring us the healing and wholeness that you alone can give, through your gracious love. Amen.

498   Living God, we bring not only the needs of others but also our own, for we are all in some way bruised, troubled in body, mind or spirit. Reach out then to all – restoring, renewing, holding, healing – and teach us to reach out also, not as the strong to the weak or the healthy to the sick but as fellow-strugglers along the journey of life, in common need of the help and wholeness that you desire for all. Amen.

499   Loving God, teach us that, though our bodies may be broken, our minds battered and our spirits crushed, you still see and value us as whole people, and, in that knowledge, may we find inner healing and tranquillity, until that day when you make us new in your eternal kingdom, through Jesus Christ our Lord. Amen.

Witnessing to Christ

By our lives

500   Sovereign God, through the power of your risen Son, continue to work within us and through us, to make your name known. Amen.

501   Gracious God, as you have so freely given your love and spoken your word to us, so teach us to share these with others, to the glory of your name. Amen.

502   Gracious God, help us to be fully involved in this world and yet to live also in the light of the world to come, and so may our lives witness to your sovereign purpose and your saving love. Amen.

503   Loving God, renew and restore us by your grace so that we may shine like stars in the world, bringing glory to you and your Father in heaven, for your name's sake. Amen.

504   Living God, help us to proclaim the gospel not just through words but through deeds – through what we say, what we do and who we are. Take what we are, and make us what we long to be, so that others, when they meet with us, may meet also with Christ and know his living presence for themselves. Amen.

505   Lord Jesus Christ, grant that everything we are, and all we say and do, may resound to your praise and glory, for your name's sake. Amen.

506   Living God, may our lips speak of you, our deeds honour you, and our lives proclaim you, through Christ our Lord. Amen.

507   Lord Jesus Christ, make us always ready to serve you, and so may we prepare the hearts of others to welcome you. Amen.

508   Lord Jesus Christ, you have touched our hearts, brought us joy and given us life in all its fullness. Equip us now, through your Spirit, to make you known and to share with others the blessing we have found in you, for your name's sake. Amen.

By our words

509   Sovereign God, you have given us so much to share, more than we can ever begin to express. You have showered us with your blessings, touching our lives in innumerable ways. Teach us to tell joyfully and spontaneously of everything you have done and all you mean to us, to the glory of your name. Amen.

510   Living God, you have given glad tidings, good news for all people. Save us from keeping it to ourselves, in the name of Christ. Amen.

511   Living God, as you have sown your word in us, help us to sow your word among others, to the glory of your name. Amen.

512   Sovereign God, whenever and wherever there is opportunity, teach us to witness in a way that is relevant and alive, speaking eagerly, faithfully and honestly of everything that you have done for us in Christ, and so may your gracious love be made known to all. Amen.

513   Lord Jesus Christ, teach me when to speak of you and when to remain silent, when to share my faith and when to leave things in your hands. Help me to know when each time may be and to respond accordingly, for your name's sake. Amen.

514   Gracious God, save us from cluttering up the gospel with our own ideas, creeds, formulas and definitions. Help us to proclaim the simple message of Christ crucified and risen, and let us leave the rest to you, in his name. Amen.

515   Lord Jesus Christ, show us when and where to speak for you, but remind us, having spoken, that you are also able to speak for yourself. Amen.

516   Lord Jesus Christ, teach us to sow the seed of your word, confident that you will nurture it until the time is ripe for harvest. Amen.

517   Living God, you call us to proclaim the gospel of Christ. Forgive us for failing to honour that calling, for being all too ready to come to you but less willing to go out in your name. Help us to recognise that, if we leave it to someone else to share the good news, they may never hear it at all. Fill us with new vision and resolve, so that, when the opportunity comes to speak for you, we may do so – faithfully, honestly, sensitively and joyfully – to the glory of your name. Amen.

518   Lord Jesus Christ, when people speak to us of you, by your grace speak through us to them, for your name's sake. Amen.

519   Lord Jesus Christ, whenever we speak for you, save us from trying to be clever; help us simply to be genuine. Amen.

520   Loving God, you have spoken to us your word of life, the good news of Jesus Christ. As we have heard, so help us to tell, for his name's sake. Amen.

521   Lord, you have given us good news to share. Help us to remember not just the message but the people you want us to share it with, and so may we speak the words you would have us say in the way you would have us say them. Amen.

522   Loving God, help us to speak your challenging, reforming and renewing word of truth, for your name's sake. Amen.

523   Loving Lord, we have so much to share – save us from ever hoarding it away. Amen.

524   Sovereign God, when you give us your word, give us the courage we need to speak it. Amen.

525   Loving God, help us to share what Christ has done for *us* so that others in turn may celebrate what he has done for *them*. In his name, we ask it. Amen.

Word of God

See also Call of God: Voice of God

526   Living God, teach us to trust that you will do everything that you have promised, your word continuing to work in our lives and in the life of the world, until your purpose has been fulfilled. Amen.

527   Living God, teach us not only to *read* the gospel but also to *live* and *share* it among all those we meet, to the glory of your name. Amen.

528   Sovereign God, as you have spoken through the Scriptures across the ages, speak also to us. Give us wisdom in reading, sensitivity in interpreting, and resolve in applying them, so that we may grow closer to you and be equipped to serve you better, to the glory of your name.

529   Loving God, for your word that has spoken to so many and continues to speak today, receive our praise, in the name of Christ. Amen.

530   Living God, teach us to read your word not as some record of past events but as a message that goes on being realised in new ways today, both in our lives and in the lives of others, by the grace of Christ. Amen.

531   Mighty and mysterious God, there is much in your word that puzzles and confuses; that sits uneasily with the good news of your love revealed in Christ and even seems to contradict it. Guide us, then, in our reading and understanding, so that we might discern what you would say to us and respond to your voice. Amen.

532   Living God, you have given us the word of life; forgive us that we fail to read it and then wonder why you fail to speak to us. Amen.

533   Living God, whether your way is easy or hard, your word comforting or disturbing, your will welcome or difficult to accept, teach us to listen, to learn and to follow faithfully, for Christ's sake. Amen.

534   Lord Jesus Christ, give us wisdom to hold on to truth but also humility to recognise that we do not have a monopoly on it. Open our hearts to your challenging and illuminating word, from wherever that might come, for your name's sake. Amen.

Worship

see also Praise

Adoration

535   Sovereign God and Father, enthroned in splendour yet here by our side, ruler of all yet friend of all, we bring our worship, we bring ourselves, praising you for your unfailing love and celebrating your great goodness. To you be honour and glory, now and always. Amen.

536   God of life, we acclaim you. God of grace, we salute you. God of power, we extol you. God of love, we praise you. Receive the worship and devotion we offer, for we bring them in joyful response and heartfelt worship. Amen.

Approach *see also* Morning

537   Sovereign God, we do not serve you as faithfully as we'd like to, we do not know you as fully as we want to, and we do not love you as much as we should do, but we long to live as your people and yearn to give you the commitment you deserve. Take, then, the discipleship we offer, flawed though it is, and work within us by your grace to make us what you would have us be, through Jesus Christ our Lord. Amen.

538   Living God, our faith is so very weak yet your love for us is so strong; our allegiance is often false yet your promises are always true; our commitment is poor yet your blessings are rich beyond words. Accept our worship and help us to honour you as freely as you bless us, every moment of every day. Amen.

539   Lord, we come not because we have to but because we want to – because we want to sing our praise, offer our adoration, express our thanks and show our love. You have blessed us beyond our deserving, enriching our lives to overflowing, and we want to tell you how grateful we are and how much you mean to us. Hear our prayer and accept our worship, in Jesus' name. Amen.

540   Mighty God, we have come again to worship you, but you, of course, are here already, close by our sides just as you have been every moment of every day, your hand upon us, your arms around us and your love within us. Open our hearts to your presence now, so that we may recognise you with us always, through Jesus Christ our Lord. Amen.

541   Living God, for welcoming us into your presence, accepting us through your grace, delighting in our worship and longing to deepen our relationship with you still further each day, we praise you. Receive our worship, which we offer you now in awe and wonder and glad thanksgiving. Amen.

542   Lord, we come to you hesitantly, overwhelmed by your greatness, yet you welcome us with arms outstretched. We come guiltily, crushed by a sense of failure, yet you pick us up and wash us clean. We come uncertainly, our faith weak and wavering, yet you are always close, eager to bless us and lead us forward into new experiences of your love. So we come – joyfully, gratefully, reverently – hungry to worship you, and once more you are here, waiting to surprise us with the wonder of your grace. Receive our praise, in Jesus' name. Amen.

Close of worship

543   Sovereign God, we have worshipped you with our lips; now let us worship you with our lives. Amen.

544   Living God, our worship is over but our service continues. Help us to offer it faithfully, every moment of every day, to the glory of your name. Amen.

545   Loving God, send us out not only with a song on our lips, but also with a song in our hearts; to the glory of your name. Amen.

546   Sovereign God, send us out in the name of Christ and the power of your Spirit. We have worshipped; now help us to serve. We have spoken; now help us to act. We have heard your word; now help us to make it known. We have rejoiced in your love; now help us to share it with others. Use us to fulfil your will and bring closer your kingdom, through Jesus Christ our Lord. Amen.

Worth of all

547   Gracious God, send us back to the world with your eyes rather than ours. Help us to see not just the bad but also the good, not simply the ugly but also the beautiful, not just the worst but also the best. Give us wisdom and discernment so that we may look beyond outward appearances to the deeper realities concealed underneath. Amen.

548   Gracious God, in all our dealings with others, help us to look for the good and bring out the best, through Jesus Christ our Lord. Amen.

549   Sovereign God, teach us that, if you can use us, you can use anyone. Amen.

550   Loving God, teach us that you value everyone not for what they might become but for what they are, and so give us a proper respect for ourselves and for all, in the name of Christ. Amen.

551   Lord of all, teach us to recognise that everyone has a place in your purpose and a contribution to make to your kingdom, and so help us to see beyond the barriers that keep us apart to everything that draws us together, through Jesus Christ our Lord. Amen.

552   Gracious God, you know what we have been, you know what we want to be, but, above all, you value what we are. May that great truth teach us to value everyone and, above all, to value you and your redeeming love in Christ. Amen.

553   Sovereign God, teach us not to think too highly of ourselves, nor too little of others. Amen.

554   Living God, teach us that *our* judgement and *yours* are rarely the same, and so awaken us to all you are able to do, through others and through us, however unlikely it may seem. Amen.

555   Creator God, teach us that you did not just make some, but all, people in your likeness, and so teach us to value and respect everyone in the family of humankind. Amen.

556   Living God, teach us to value both others and ourselves as much as *you* value us all. Teach us to respect what it means to be human and so to consecrate everything that we are to your service, in the name of Christ. Amen.

557   Lord Jesus Christ, as you have seen the good in us, so help us to see the good in others, for your name's sake. Amen.

558   Loving God, send us out rejoicing in the knowledge that you value us, and help us to show how much we value others, expressing our concern and appreciation through word and deed, to the glory of your name. Amen.

559   Sovereign God, give us a deeper awareness of your greatness and a fuller appreciation of the worth of those around us. Grant us a proper sense of our own importance, neither valuing ourselves too little nor too highly. In the name of Christ we ask it. Amen.

560   Gracious God, give us a proper sense of our own worth, a true appreciation of the worth of others, and, above all, an understanding of your greatness, beside which we are as nothing, yet through which you count us your children. Amen.

561   Sovereign God, you recognise the potential of everyone and everything; help us to do the same. Amen.